Descendants of Ambrose Newton Edwards

Generation 1

1. **AMBROSE NEWTON**[1] **EDWARDS** was born on 21 Oct 1840 in Russell County, Alabama. He died on 20 Jul 1933 in Strawn, Texas. He married Joanna Columbia Ardis, daughter of Isaac Ardis and Jane Elizabeth White on 05 Dec 1865 in Dale County, Alabama. She was born on 04 Feb 1847 in Salem, Alabama. She died on 08 Aug 1922 in Greenville, Texas.

More About Ambrose Newton Edwards:
Burial: 21 Jul 1933 in Forest Park Cemetery, Greenville, Texas- Moved later to Restland Cemetery, Dallas, Texas
Cause Of Death: Prostate Cancer
Occupation: 1860 in Dale County, Alabama; School Teacher
Occupation: 1870 in Sulphur Springs, Texas; Dry Goods Merchant
Occupation: 1880 in Hopkins County, Texas; County Clerk
Occupation: Bet. 27 Mar 1886-20 Oct 1891 ; Postmaster, Eliasville, Texas
Occupation: 1900 in Palo Pinto County, Texas; Lumber Dealer
Occupation: 1910 in Gordon, Palo Pinto County, Texas; Lumber Merchant
Occupation: 1920 in Palo Pinto County, Texas; Retired
Occupation: 1930 in Greenville, Texas; Retired - Living with his son, Ambrose Edwin Edwards
Military Service: Bet. 03 Jul 1861-11 Jun 1865; Company E, 15th Alabama Infantry, C.S.A.

Notes for Ambrose Newton Edwards:
    Enlisted on July 3, 1861 in Westville, Alabama and served until July 2, 1863 when he was captured at Gettysburg, Pennsylvania and made a prisoner of war. Sent first to Fort McHenry, Maryland on July 5, 1863 and then to Fort Delaware, Delaware on July 6, 1863. Released from Fort Delaware on June 11, 1865
    Engagements: Winchester, Cross Keys, Harpers Ferry, Sharpsburg, Fredricksburg, Suffolk, Malvern Hill, Cedar Mt. Hazel River, 2nd Manassas, Chantilly, Gettysburg.

    Wounded at Sharpsburg.and Fredricksburg.

    Promoted to Second Sergeant May 15, 1862.
    Promoted to First Sergeant July 25, 1862.
    Promoted to Second Lieutenant but was captured at Gettysburg, Pennsylvania before his commission arrived.

    Pre Civil War Residence was Westville, Alabama.

    Flag of the Army of Northern Virginia covered his casket during his first funeral and burial at Greeneville, Texas.

    Member of the first Board of Regents for the University of Texas 1881-1882

    Buried in Greenville, Texas in 1933 and then buried in Restland Cemetery, Dallas, Texas on February 9, 1955, grave marker set on August 31, 1955.

    Became a Mason at Brightstar Lodge number 221 in Sulphur Springs, Texas on November 5, 1868.

    Death certificate gives October 18, 1840 as date of birth.

    Dictated to Emma Irene Garland (Edwards) in 1930

    I well remember the day when my company assembled at old Darian Church in Dale County,

Alabama, where we bade good bye to our loved ones and took up our march to the battle front in answer to our country's call.

I remember the first night we camped on the banks of Pea River and bathed in its waters and spent this our first night in joyous hilarity. I remember after three days march we reached old Fort Mitchell near Columbus Georgia, where we were organized into the 15th Alabama Infantry, my company being known as co. E. Then after a few weeks of company and regimental drill we had orders to go to Virginia, and this was for me a matter of exquisite thrill and interest which cannot be well depicted here.

When we reached Richmond we were quartered at Old Chimborozo where we remained about three weeks and thence to Manassas. Shortly after the noted first battle of the war, as there was no more fighting in this section, we went into winter quarters there. Up to this time we had not had to suffer any great hardships, but had many interesting experiences.

In the beginning of 1862, the second year of the war, greater activities in war matters became more tense. McClelland was assembling a great army in the Yorktown peninsula with the purpose of marching on to Richmond and General Johnson was ordered to fall back from Manassas to meet this move of the enemy. But Ewell's division, to which I belonged, was ordered to join Stonewall Jackson in the valley. Then my regiment was in the noted Valley campaign in which Jackson defeated three armies and then it was at Cross Keys we received our baptism of battle. From here the scene changed and the Seven days battle around Richmond was fought in which my regiment took an active part and lost quite a number of noble men.

I was sick and in the hospital at Charlottesville at that time. After McClelland's defeat General Lee moved his army North. On the first invasion. we crossed the Potomac at Leesburg, wading it of course as there were no bridges. My division was ordered to go around and cross back above Harper's Ferry where General Wool was stationed with seven thousand men. We had him completely surrounded and he surrendered. In this surrender we secured arms, commissary, and quarter master supplies in great abundance.

Immediately after the surrender we were ordered back across the Potomac to be in the battle of Sharpsburg - called Antetim by the North Historians - this was one of the hardest battles of the war, and was known as a draw. Lee withdrew to the Virginia side and there ended that year's campaign in Virginia.

To avoid being tedious, I will omit many important military operations including the battle of Fredricksburg in which i took a part and will speak of the Pennsylvania invasion and the battle of Gettysburg. I was in this battle and on the second day of July 1863, with thirteen other men of my company was captured and carried to Fort Delaware where we were kept as prisoners until the war closed.

I could make an interesting chapter about our prison, but only say we managed to keep up spirit and hope amid its trials and troubles until the day came for our release nearly two months after the surrender.

I reached home on the 5th of June 1865, to find our beloved Southland wrecked and ruined by war's devastation.

Then it was with unflinching courage we took up the task of reconstructing the ruin and building our new South upon it. While I cannot elaborate on this work, for it would require many words, yet I cannot omit saying that the work was done in a way that solicited the admiration of all people. Our noble women were our staunch co-laborers in every sence, and deserve a monument for their wonderful work.

On the 5th of December 1865 it was my good fortune to lead to the marriage alter one of the best of the noble daughters of the South, to walk with me and share with me, every joy and every sorrow that awaited us on lifes pilgrimage. We came to Texas in 1866 where eight sons came to bless our union, all noble men and all living useful lives in Texas except one. Eight years ago my precious one left me to go and wear her crown.

Now in my 90th year I can truly say that much love and kindness have been meted out to me, but must say that the best friends we old veterans have are the noble Daughters of the Confederacy, and may god bless them in my closing word.

A. N. Edwards
Co. E. 15th Alabama Inf.

More About Joanna Columbia Ardis:
Burial: 08 Aug 1922 in Forest Park Cemetery, Greenville, Texas- Moved later to
Restland Cemetery, Dallas, Texas
Cause Of Death: Stomach Cancer

Notes for Joanna Columbia Ardis:
Re buried in Restland Cemetery, Dallas, Texas on February 9, 1955, grave marker set on
August 31, 1955.

Relationship Notes for Ambrose Newton Edwards and Joanna Columbia Ardis:
Ambrose and Joanna were married in a double ceremony with Young Mansfield Edwards
and Martha Ardis.

Ambrose Newton Edwards and Joanna Columbia Ardis had the following children:

2.   i. ISAAC MANSFIELD[2] EDWARDS was born on 01 Feb 1868 in Strawn, Texas. He died on 18
Mar 1945 in Strawn Texas. He married Mary Sophronia (Onie) Strawn, daughter of
Stephen Bethel Strawn and Emeline Jane Allen in 1899 in Palo Pinto County, Texas.
She was born on 11 Apr 1874 in Strawn, Texas. She died on 18 Feb 1950 in Temple,
Bell County, Texas.

ii.   WALTER WHITE EDWARDS was born on 31 Oct 1870 in Sulphur Springs, Texas. He
died on 27 Nov 1938 in El Paso, Texas. He married Mary Anna King, daughter
of Porter King and Eudorah Martha Bush in 1897 in Palo Pinto County, Texas.
She was born on 23 Jul 1864 in Texas. She died on 23 Dec 1956 in Amarillo,
Potter County, Texas.

More About Walter White Edwards:
Burial: 29 Nov 1938 in Evergreen Cemetery, El Paso,
Texas Cause Of Death: Cardiac Failure, Hypertension
Occupation: 1910; Gold Miner, Gorden, Palo Pinto County,
Texas Occupation: 1920; Salesman, El Paso, Texas
Occupation: 1930; Geologist, El Paso, Texas

Notes for Walter White
Edwards: Dear Mr. Edwards:
Your request to our Geological Information Center for information on the
Baking Powder mine was forwarded to me. Probably fewer than a half-dozen
living people in all the southwest have even heard of
this property as it is one of the more obscure such in all New Mexico. I am not
aware that the property was ever examined by a trained geologist or engineer
(unless your Edwards relatives were such and there is no known surviving record
of their work). My extensive mines and prospects files are absolutely silent in
regard to the Baking Powder. Nevertheless I have noted one or two very obscure
references in my research.
The Baking Powder is located in the Rosedale Mining District at the extreme
north end of the San Mateo mountains in southern Socorro county, New Mexico. I

have not examined the mining claim records in the local courthouse for exact dates (mainly because you are the very first individual to ever request information on the property!) but would predict the claim (or claims) was located during latter part of the 19th century -- poss. mid-1890s -- as a result of the success of the well-known Rosedale mine and discovery of the nearby White Cap.

The "veins" in the Rosedale district are actually brecciated shear zones in the volcanic (rhyolitic) rocks The brecciated and sheared rhyolite has been recemented with a hard, bluish-white quartz and later with a clearer vein-type quartz. The entire vein mass is highly silicified and in those areas yielding the best gold values are heavily stained with the black and red oxides of manganese and iron respectively. Gold occurred in the native state in the upper oxidized portions of the vein but is very nearly absent in the sulfide portion at or below the water table. Remarkably, little or no silver is present. I would predict the Baking Powder "vein" to be similar in character to the above. Dr. Charles Ferguson's doctoral dissertation covered a large area extending from the southern end of the Rosedale District to the north well beyond White Cap and Big Rosa canyons. I asked Charlie if he knew the locality of the Baking Powder and other prospects and he indicated approximate locations for two unnamed mine workings about two miles north and northwest of the Rosedale which I feel are the White Cap and the Baking Powder. The projected location for the latter is approx. Sec3, T6S, R6W near the head of Big Rosa canyon.

Soon after the turn of the century, development on the Baking Powder had apparently progressed to the mining stage. According to a note in the Engineering and Mining Journal, 24 December 1903, p 988, the Baking Powder mine was said to be initiating "full operations," whatever that meant; Walter Edwards, undoubtedly your ancestor, was the manager. Unfortunately the operation failed to live up to expectations and within four years was facing foreclosure for $1200 in back wages (Soccoro Chieftan, 30 November 1907). The obvious conclusion is that the mine failed to develop pay ore in sufficient quantities to sustain the operation and it failed. And that is the current extent of the "historic" record!

I and my colleagues attempted to visit this prospect in May 2000, but despite our "approximate" location on the topo sheet, and a full day's search, four-wheeling, etc., we failed to locate it. I should note that the 'road' up Big Rosa canyon is, in places, a figment of the imagination -- we could have easily missed a small prospect off in the ponderosas! The Mount Whithington jeep road may pass within a mile of the mine on the west and that is the route I will next attempt.

Now that you have made a request for information, I shall keep a sharp lookout for additional data. I must yet peruse the pages of the few issues of the San Marcial Bee that have survived the ravages of time and will keep you in mind should anything materialize. Additionally I will examine the claim location records upon my next visit to the courthouse. On the other hand, I'd be most pleased to add to our archival files any information you'd be willing to share with us from your family's papers. Regards,

Robert W. Eveleth Senior
Mining Engineer Curator,
Mining Archives

Dear Mr. Edwards:

Recent research on several articles of local mining interest has, once again, led me through the pages of the Socorro Chieftain. Recalling your interest in the above, I made a copy of an article on the Baking Powder/Edwards Bros., reproduced below in its entirety:

Socorro Chieftain, 6/14/1902, p 4: "Rosedale, N. M., June 10m, 1902 -- Editor Chieftain -- Rosedale is quiet at present. Big Rosa, 2-1/2 miles to the northwest, shows great and rapidly increasing activity. Fully $5,000 worth of work is now underway and other contracts are being let. The immediate cause of this work was the discovery and partial development of the Baking Powder property of the Edwards Brothers of El Paso, Tex. This claim showed well from the surface but now at a depth of 55 feet it is exciting old time prospectors and tenderfeet alike by yielding a strong vein of high grade ore while picked samples show as high as 84 ounces in gold. Two or more stamp mills, stores, drink emporiums, a post office, dozens of cabins and tents, a good graded road up Big Rosa, and a couple of hundred men tearing into its mountain sides may be a vision, but as a miner and prospector of long experience I think this and more will be a reality within 12 months. Big Rosa may not be as good a mining camp as Cripple Creek, Colo. It may be better. The writer has no interest there and is not puffing the camp to "induce capital," but is sincere in saying that right now is a suitable and very favorable time to investigate Big Rosa.

There can be no harm in keeping an eye on the indicator." Signed: A. L. Heister."

As I continue to go through the pages of the Socorro Chieftan, I'll be sure to let you know if the writer's dream materialized.

Best Regards,
Robert W. Eveleth
Senior Mining Engineer

----

3.   iii. AMBROSE EDWIN EDWARDS was born on 20 Mar 1872 in Sulphur Springs, Texas. He died on 15 Feb 1963 in Dallas, Texas. He married Anne Buntin Yarbrough, daughter of George Yarbrough and Margaret Augusta Herrin on 03 Jul 1901 in Grayson County, Texas. She was born on 15 Oct 1871 in Tyler, Texas. She died on 24 Oct 1955 in Dallas, Texas.

       v. MARVIN M. EDWARDS was born on 28 Nov 1875 in Riley Springs, Texas. He died on 11 Sep 1900 in Strawn, Texas.

More About Marvin M. Edwards:
Burial: Mount Marion Cemetery, Strawn, Texas
Cause Of Death: Consumption (Tuberculosis)
Living In: 1900 Palo Pinto County, Texas with his parents

4.   v. MCDONALD EDWARDS was born on 10 Dec 1877 in Strawn, Texas. He died on 08 Nov 1957 in Lubbock, Texas. He married Sally May Marchbanks, daughter of Finley W. Marchbanks and Sarah A. Hix on 26 Feb 1899 in Strawn, Texas. She was born on 12 Feb 1877 in Cleburne, Texas. She died on 27 Oct 1957 in Fort Worth, Texas.

5.   vi. LEROY ARDIS EDWARDS was born on 27 Feb 1881 in Sulphur Springs, Texas. He died on 05 Dec 1951 in Loraine, Texas. He married (1) EMMA GEORGIE IRENE GARLAND, daughter of Edward Warren Garland and Julia Rebecca Kimbell on 27 Jul 1921 in Roscoe, Texas. She was born on 23 Mar 1880 in Annona, Texas. She died on 17 Dec 1969 in Kerrville, Texas. He married (2) ADA MAY LOFLIN, daughter of Daniel Vance Loflin and Margarite Sophia Crawley on 21 Nov 1906 in Palo Pinto County, Texas. She was born on 26 Apr 1886 in Palo Pinto County, Texas. She died on 15 Apr 1918 in Loraine, Texas.

6.   vii. BECTON GOODSON EDWARDS was born on 29 Oct 1884 in Sulphur Springs, Texas. He died on 04 Dec 1960 in Dallas, Dallas County, Texas. He married Minnie Mae Strain, daughter of George Douglas Strain and Sarah Elizabeth Strawn on 04 Nov

1908 in Weatherford, Texas. She was born on 22 Feb 1887 in Strawn, Texas. She died on 28 Jul 1956 in Corsicana, Navarro County, Texas.

viii. JOHN MCTYEIRE EDWARDS was born on 08 Dec 1888 in Eliasville, Texas. He died on 05 Oct 1970 in Killeen, Texas.

More About John McTyeire Edwards:
Burial: 09 Oct 1970 in Fort Sam Houston National Cemetery, San Antonio, Texas Cause Of Death: Acute Myocardio Infarction, Generalized Arteriosclerosis
Living In: 1910 Greenville, Texas
Occupation: 1920 in Palo Pinto County, Texas; Bank Cashier
Occupation: 1930 in San Antonio, Texas; Hotel Clerk
Occupation: 1940 in San Antonio, Texas; Private Residence Gardener
Military Service: Bet. 19 Sep 1917-24 Mar 1919; Sergeant First Class, World War One

Notes for John McTyeire
Edwards: Never Married

Probably named after John McTyeire of Russell County, Alabama.

Served in HQ Company, 165th Depot Brigade, U.S. Army

Generation 2

2. ISAAC MANSFIELD^2 EDWARDS (Ambrose Newton^1) was born on 01 Feb 1868 in Strawn, Texas. He died on 18 Mar 1945 in Strawn Texas. He married Mary Sophronia (Onie) Strawn, daughter of Stephen Bethel Strawn and Emeline Jane Allen in 1899 in Palo Pinto County, Texas. She was born on 11 Apr 1874 in Strawn, Texas. She died on 18 Feb 1950 in Temple, Bell County, Texas.

More About Isaac Mansfield Edwards:
Burial: 19 Mar 1945 in Mount Marion Cemetery, Strawn, Texas
Cause Of Death: Coronary Thrombosis and Embolism
Occupation: 1900 in Palo Pinto County, Texas; Farmer
Occupation: 1910 in Strawn, Texas; Carpenter
Occupation: 1920 in Weatherford, Texas; Carpenter
Occupation: 1930 in Strawn, Texas; Painter
Occupation: 1940 in Strawn, Texas; Painter

Notes for Isaac Mansfield Edwards:
Death certificate gives date of birth as February 1, 1868. 1900 U.S. census gives date of birth as February 1868. Headstone gives date of birth as February 1, 1870.

More About Mary Sophronia (Onie) Strawn:
Burial: 18 Feb 1950 in Mount Marion Cemetery, Strawn, Texas Cause Of Death: Obstructive Jaundice

Notes for Mary Sophronia (Onie) Strawn:
Death certificate gives date of birth as April 11, 1874. 1900 U.S. census gives date of birth as April 1874. Headstone gives date of birth as April 11, 1875.

Isaac Mansfield Edwards and Mary Sophronia (Onie) Strawn had the following children:

7.   i.   MURRAY ARDIS[3] EDWARDS was born on 05 Jul 1900 in Strawn, Texas. He died on 16 Aug 1944 in Dallas, Texas. He married Johnie Belle Burt, daughter of John Frederick Burt and Anna Belle Miller on 25 May 1922. She was born on 02 May 1898. She died on 20 Jan 1986 in Tarrant County, Texas.

8.   ii.   ALLEN NEWTON EDWARDS was born on 24 Apr 1902 in Texas. He died in Feb 1979 in Tulsa, Oklahoma. He married ALLIE EDITH HERRIN. She was born on 13 Feb 1905. She died in Feb 1991.

      iii. CHARLES EDWARDS.

3.   **AMBROSE EDWIN[2] EDWARDS** (Ambrose Newton[1]) was born on 20 Mar 1872 in Sulphur Springs, Texas. He died on 15 Feb 1963 in Dallas, Texas. He married Anne Buntin Yarbrough, daughter of George Yarbrough and Margaret Augusta Herrin on 03 Jul 1901 in Grayson County, Texas. She was born on 15 Oct 1871 in Tyler, Texas. She died on 24 Oct 1955 in Dallas, Texas.

More About Ambrose Edwin Edwards:
Burial: 18 Feb 1963 in Restland Cemetery, Dallas,
Texas Cause Of Death: Cerebral Arteriosclerosis
Occupation: 1910 in Greenville, Texas; Real Estate Agent
Occupation: 1920 in Greenville, Texas; Real Estate Agent
Occupation: 1930 in Greenville, Texas; Farm Loan Agent
Occupation: 1940 in Dallas, Texas; Real Estate Proprietor

Notes for Ambrose Edwin Edwards:
Middle name of Edwin is probably after Doctor Edwin P. Becton of Sulphur Springs, Texas.

 Birth date is from Social Security death index. Headstone has 1871 for year of birth but this would conflict with the birth date of his brother, Walter White Edwards.

More About Anne Buntin Yarbrough:
Burial: 25 Oct 1955 in Restland Cemetery, Dallas, Texas
Cause Of Death: ; Coronary Occlusion

Ambrose Edwin Edwards and Anne Buntin Yarbrough had the following children:

9.   i.   AMBROSE YARBROUGH[3] EDWARDS was born on 16 Sep 1904 in Greeneville, Texas. He died on 18 Mar 1999 in Dallas, Texas. He married Mary Ruth Howell, daughter of Zebbie Lee Howell and Laura Annie Middleton on 09 Aug 1935 in Greenville, Texas. She was born on 06 Sep 1905 in Richland, Texas. She died on 31 Dec 1998.

10.   ii.   GEORGE NEWTON EDWARDS was born on 01 May 1908 in Texas. He died on 28 Apr 1955 in University Park, Dallas County, Texas. He married THERESA BRYAN. She was born on 10 Sep 1907. She died on 29 Jul 1992.

4.   **MCDONALD[2] EDWARDS** (Ambrose Newton[1]) was born on 10 Dec 1877 in Strawn, Texas. He died on 8 Nov 1957 in Lubbock, Texas. He married Sally May Marchbanks, daughter of Finley W. Marchbanks and Sarah A. Hix on 26 Feb 1899 in Strawn, Texas. She was born on 12 Feb 1877 in Cleburne, Texas. She died on 27 Oct 1957 in Fort Worth, Texas.

More About McDonald Edwards:
Burial: 08 Nov 1957 in O'Donnell Cemetery, O'Donnell, Texas

Cause Of Death: Nephrosclerosis
Occupation: 1900 in Palo Pinto County, Texas; Hack Man
Occupation: 1910 in Palo Pinto County, Texas; Lumber Merchant
Occupation: 1920 in Palo Pinto County, Texas; Lumber Merchant
Occupation: 1930 in O'Donnell, Texas; Lumber Yard Manager
Occupation: 1940 in O'Donnell, Texas; Lumber Yard Proprietor

More About Sally May Marchbanks:
Burial: 28 Oct 1957 in O'Donnell Cemetery, O'Donnell, Texas
Cause Of Death: Chronic Myocarditis

Notes for Sally May Marchbanks:
Headstone gives name as Sallie May instead of Sally May.

McDonald Edwards and Sally May Marchbanks had the following children:

11.　　i. MARION WIRT[3] EDWARDS was born on 24 Aug 1901 in Strawn, Texas. He died on 07 Sep 1971 in Arlington, Tarrant County, Texas. He married Mary Elizabeth Gray on 30 Apr 1938 in Arlington, Texas. She was born on 18 Sep 1910 in Dallas, Texas. She died in 1999.

　　　ii. LOUISE EDWARDS was born about 1913 in Texas. She married WILBER LINE.

5.　LEROY ARDIS[2] EDWARDS (Ambrose Newton[1]) was born on 27 Feb 1881 in Sulphur Springs, Texas. He died on 05 Dec 1951 in Loraine, Texas. He married (1) EMMA GEORGIE IRENE GARLAND, daughter of Edward Warren Garland and Julia Rebecca Kimbell on 27 Jul 1921 in Roscoe, Texas. She was born on 23 Mar 1880 in Annona, Texas. She died on 17 Dec 1969 in Kerrville, Texas. He married (2) ADA MAY LOFLIN, daughter of Daniel Vance Loflin and Margarite Sophia Crawley on 21 Nov 1906 in Palo Pinto County, Texas. She was born on 26 Apr 1886 in Palo Pinto County, Texas. She died on 15 Apr 1918 in Loraine, Texas.

More About LeRoy Ardis Edwards:
Burial: 07 Dec 1951 in Loraine Cemetery, Loraine,
Texas Cause Of Death: Carcinoma of Lung
Occupation: 1910 in Brazoria County, Texas; Truck Farmer
Occupation: 1918 in Ranger, Eastland County, Texas; Manager of Buell Lumber Company
Occupation: 1920 in Loraine, Texas; Lumber Yard Manager
Occupation: 1930 in Loraine, Texas; Lumber Yard Manager
Occupation: 1940 in Olton, Texas; Retail Lumber Yard Manager
Occupation: 1942 in Olton, Lamb County, Texas; Manager of Higgingbotham Lumber

Company Notes for LeRoy Ardis Edwards:

Discovered and operated, with his brother Walter, "Baking Powder" gold mine near Rosedale, New Mexico.

Dear Mr. Edwards:
Your request to our Geological Information Center for information on the Baking Powder mine was forwarded to me. Probably fewer than a half-dozen living people in all the southwest have even heard of
this property as it is one of the more obscure such in all New Mexico. I am not aware that the

property was ever examined by a trained geologist or engineer (unless your Edwards relatives were such and there is no known surviving record of their work). My extensive mines and prospects files are absolutely silent in regard to the Baking Powder. Nevertheless I have noted one or two very obscure references in my research.

The Baking Powder is located in the Rosedale Mining District at the extreme north end of the San Mateo mountains in southern Socorro county, New Mexico. I have not examined the mining claim records in the local courthouse for exact dates (mainly because you are the very first individual to ever request information on the property!) but would predict the claim (or claims) was located during latter part of the 19th century -- poss. mid-1890s -- as a result of the success of the well-known Rosedale mine and discovery of the nearby White Cap.

The "veins" in the Rosedale district are actually brecciated shear zones in the volcanic (rhyolitic) rocks The brecciated and sheared rhyolite has been recemented with a hard, bluish-white quartz and later with a clearer vein-type quartz. The entire vein mass is highly silicified and in those areas yielding the best gold values are heavily stained with the black and red oxides of manganese and iron respectively. Gold occurred in the native state in the upper oxidized portions of the vein but is very nearly absent in the sulfide portion at or below the water table. Remarkably, little or no silver is present. I would predict the Baking Powder "vein" to be similar in character to the above. Dr. Charles Ferguson's doctoral dissertation covered a large area extending from the southern end of the Rosedale District to the north well beyond White Cap and Big Rosa canyons. I asked Charlie if he knew the locality of the Baking Powder and other prospects and he indicated approximate locations for two unnamed mine workings about two miles north and northwest of the Rosedale which I feel are the White Cap and the Baking Powder. The projected location for the latter is approx. Sec3, T6S, R6W near the head of Big Rosa canyon.

Soon after the turn of the century, development on the Baking Powder had apparently progressed to the mining stage. According to a note in the Engineering and Mining Journal, 24 December 1903, p 988, the Baking Powder mine was said to be initiating "full operations," whatever that meant; Walter Edwards, undoubtedly your ancestor, was the manager. Unfortunately the operation failed to live up to expectations and within four years was facing foreclosure for $1200 in back wages (Soccoro Chieftan, 30 November 1907). The obvious conclusion is that the mine failed to develop pay ore in sufficient quantities to sustain the operation and it failed. And that is the current extent of the "historic" record!

I and my colleagues attempted to visit this prospect in May 2000, but despite our "approximate" location on the topo sheet, and a full day's search, four-wheeling, etc., we failed to locate it. I should note that the 'road' up Big Rosa canyon is, in places, a figment of the imagination -- we could have easily missed a small prospect off in the ponderosas! The Mount Whithington jeep road may pass within a mile of the mine on the west and that is the route I will next attempt.

Now that you have made a request for information, I shall keep a sharp lookout for additional data. I must yet peruse the pages of the few issues of the San Marcial Bee that have survived the ravages of time and will keep you in mind should anything materialize. Additionally I will examine the claim location records upon my next visit to the courthouse. On the other hand, I'd be most pleased to add to our archival files any information you'd be willing to share with us from your family's papers. Regards,

Robert W. Eveleth Senior
Mining Engineer Curator,
Mining Archives

Dear Mr. Edwards:

Recent research on several articles of local mining interest has, once again, led me through the pages of the Socorro Chieftain. Recalling your interest in the above, I made a copy of an article on the Baking Powder/Edwards Bros., reproduced below in its entirety:

Socorro Chieftain, 6/14/1902, p 4: "Rosedale, N. M., June 10m, 1902 -- Editor Chieftain -- Rosedale is quiet at present. Big Rosa, 2-1/2 miles to the northwest, shows great and rapidly increasing activity. Fully $5,000 worth of work is now underway and other contracts are being let. The immediate cause of this work was the discovery and partial development of the Baking Powder property of the Edwards Brothers of El Paso, Tex. This claim showed well from the surface but now at a depth of 55 feet it is exciting old time prospectors and tenderfeet alike by yielding a strong vein of high grade ore while picked samples show as high as 84 ounces in gold. Two or more stamp mills, stores, drink emporiums, a post office, dozens of cabins and tents, a good graded road up Big Rosa, and a couple of hundred men tearing into its mountain sides may be a vision, but as a miner and prospector of long experience I think this and more will be a reality within 12 months. Big Rosa may not be as good a mining camp as Cripple Creek, Colo. It may be better. The writer has no interest there and is not puffing the camp to "induce capital," but is sincere in saying that right now is a suitable and very favorable time to investigate Big Rosa.

There can be no harm in keeping an eye on the indicator." Signed: A. L. Heister."

As I continue to go through the pages of the Socorro Chieftan, I'll be sure to let you know if the writer's dream materialized.

Best Regards,
Robert W. Eveleth
Senior Mining Engineer

-- ----

More About Emma Georgie Irene Garland:
Burial: 20 Dec 1969 in Loraine Cemetery, Loraine, Texas
Cause Of Death: Bronchial Pneumonia and Arteriosclerosis

More About LeRoy Ardis Edwards and Emma Georgie Irene Garland:
Marriage License: 27 Jul 1921 in Mitchell County, Texas
Marriage Fact: Married by S. H. Young, M.G.

LeRoy Ardis Edwards and Emma Georgie Irene Garland had the following child:

12.   i.   ROY GARLAND[3] EDWARDS was born on 30 May 1922 in Loraine, Texas. He died on 14 Oct 1974 in Tampa, Florida. He married Maribel Savage, daughter of William Payne Savage and Mary Bell Badgett on 08 Apr 1944 in Lubbock, Texas. She was born on 22 Jun 1926 in Sherman, Texas. She died on 14 Feb 2010 in Tampa, Florida.

More About Ada May Loflin:
Burial: Mount Marion Cemetery, Strawn, Texas

LeRoy Ardis Edwards and Ada May Loflin had the following children:

13.   ii.   ESTHA LOUISE EDWARDS was born on 07 Apr 1908 in Ranger, Texas. She died on 23 May 1994 in Abilene, Texas. She married Floyd Franklin Coffee, son of Thomas Joshua Coffee and Hannah Pauline Dorn on 24 Aug 1934 in Snyder, Texas. He was born on 01 Dec 1900 in Mitchell County, Texas. He died on 19 Feb 1994 in Loraine, Texas.

14.   iii.   MARVIN YOUNG EDWARDS was born on 20 Sep 1910 in Alvin, Texas. He died on 19 Jan 1985 in Abilene, Texas. He married (1) EVELYN VIRGINIA COX, daughter of Bluford Sanford Cox and Mary Maud Baze on 15 Jun 1935 in Mitchell County, Texas. She was born on 11 May 1913 in Bay City, Texas. She died on 16 Feb 1979 in Abilene, Taylor County, Texas. He married (2) LAURA ALICE FERGUSON, daughter of Charles C. Ferguson and Annie Ruth Martin on 24 Sep 1981 in Jones County, Texas. She was born on 21 Sep 1919 in McCaulley, Fisher County, Texas. She died on 26 Jul 1994 in Abilene, Texas.

15.   iv.   MARGARET RUTH EDWARDS was born on 18 Jan 1917 in Loraine, Texas. She died

on 26 Dec 1984 in Tempe, Arizona. She married William Glenn Johnson, son of Edgar Francis Johnson and Ada Eva Jennings on 25 Sep 1939 in Phoenix, Arizona. He was born on 12 Aug 1910 in Statesville, Tennessee. He died on 28 Jan 1988 in Tempe, Arizona.

6.   **BECTON GOODSON[2] EDWARDS** (Ambrose Newton[1]) was born on 29 Oct 1884 in Sulphur Springs, Texas. He died on 04 Dec 1960 in Dallas, Dallas County, Texas. He married Minnie Mae Strain, daughter of George Douglas Strain and Sarah Elizabeth Strawn on 04 Nov 1908 in Weatherford, Texas. She was born on 22 Feb 1887 in Strawn, Texas. She died on 28 Jul 1956 in Corsicana, Navarro County, Texas.

More About Becton Goodson Edwards:
Burial: 06 Dec 1960 in Grove Hill Cemetery, Dallas, Dallas County, Texas
Cause Of Death: Coronary Occlusion, Arteriosclerosis Heart Valve
Occupation: 1910 in Weatherford, Texas; Real Estate and Insurance Salesman
Occupation: 1920 in Forney, Texas; Postmaster
Occupation: 1930 in Forney, Texas; Pharmacist
Occupation: 1940 in Forney, Texas; Retail Drug Store Manager

Notes for Becton Goodson Edwards:
Named after Doctor Edwin P. Becton of Sulphur Springs, Texas. Doctor Becton served in the 22nd Texas Infantry, C.S.A., during the Civil War and is buried in Sulphur Springs City Cemetery, Sulphur Springs, Texas.

More About Minnie Mae Strain:
Burial: 28 Jul 1956 in Grove Hill Cemetery, Dallas, Dallas County, Texas
Cause Of Death: Cerebral Hemorrhage

Notes for Minnie Mae Strain:
Death certificate has her middle name spelled "May". Headstone has her middle name spelled "Mae".

More About Becton Goodson Edwards and Minnie Mae Strain:
Marriage License: 03 Nov 1908 in Parker County, Texas
Marriage Fact: Married by George M. Oakley, Minister of the Gospel

Becton Goodson Edwards and Minnie Mae Strain had the following children:

    i.   LOIS ELIZABETH[3] EDWARDS was born on 16 Sep 1909 in Texas. She died on 08 Jul 1993 in Bexar County, Texas. She married (UNKNOWN) WADE.

        More About Lois Elizabeth Edwards:
        Living In: 1993 in San Antonio, Bexar County, Texas
        Occupation: 1930 in Forney, Texas; Public School Teacher

    ii.   ERNEST WELDON EDWARDS was born on 03 Dec 1910 in Texas. He died on 15 Mar 1945 on the Island of Iwo Jima. He married MARIE GARRETT. She was born on 08 Feb 1908 in Texas. She died on 18 Nov 1950 in Dallas, Dallas County, Texas.

        More About Ernest Weldon Edwards:

Burial: 21 Mar 1949 in National Memorial Cemetery of the Pacific.
Living In: 1935 Dallas, Dallas County, Texas
Occupation: 1930 in Forney, Texas; Garage Mechanic
Occupation: 1940 in Dallas, Dallas County, Texas; Sandwich Shop Manager
Military Service: United States Marine Corps, World War Two

Notes for Ernest Weldon Edwards:
Died during the assault of Iwo Jima in World war Two.

Graduate of SMU.

16.   iii. RUTH EDWARDS was born on 10 Aug 1912 in Tyler, Texas. She died on 05 Sep 2004 in Dallas, Texas. She married Albert Lee Greer in 1938. He was born on 04 Apr 1911 in Dallas, Texas. He died on 09 Nov 2001 in Dallas, Texas.

      iv. GEORGE ARDIS EDWARDS was born on 16 Jul 1914 in Forney, Texas. He died on 13 Nov 1953 in Austin, Travis County, Texas.

More About George Ardis Edwards:
Burial: Grove Hill Memorial Park, Dallas, Dallas County, Texas
Cause Of Death: Coronary Occlusions
Living In: 1953 Dallas, Dallas County, Texas
Occupation: Accountant Clerk with Power and Light Company
Military Service: U.S. Navy - World War Two

17.   v. MARVIN BECTON EDWARDS was born on 22 Nov 1923 in Texas. He died on 01 Feb 1973. He married Patricia Ann White on 25 Jun 1946 in Terrell County, Texas. She was born on 03 Mar 1928 in Terrell County, Texas. She died in Jan 2003 in Longview, Texas.

18.   vi. MARGARET ANNE EDWARDS was born on 04 Sep 1929 in Forney, Kaufman County, Texas. She died on 17 Jun 2011 in Silsbee, Texas. She married (1) JOHN PATRICK MOONEYHAM, son of Jesse Mooneyham and Hazel N. Easterly on 24 Sep 1947. He was born on 17 Mar 1929 in Kemp, Texas. He died on 23 Oct 2000 in Silsbee, Texas. She married (2) ROBERT RAY ROBINSON on 28 Feb 1981 in Jefferson County, Texas. He was born on 10 Jun 1944. He died on 28 Sep 2005 in Beaumont, Texas.

Generation 3

7. MURRAY ARDIS[3] EDWARDS (Isaac Mansfield[2], Ambrose Newton[1]) was born on 05 Jul 1900 in Strawn, Texas. He died on 16 Aug 1944 in Dallas, Texas. He married Johnie Belle Burt, daughter of John Frederick Burt and Anna Belle Miller on 25 May 1922. She was born on 02 May 1898. She died on 20 Jan 1986 in Tarrant County, Texas.

More About Murray Ardis Edwards:
Burial: 16 Aug 1944 in Mount Marion Cemetery, Strawn, Texas
Cause Of Death: Brain Tumor - benign
Occupation: 1930 Bank Cashier, Loraine, Texas
Occupation: 1944 Collector for Internal Revenue Service

More About Johnie Belle Burt:
Burial: Mount Marion Cemetery, Strawn, Texas

Murray Ardis Edwards and Johnie Belle Burt had the following child:

19.   i. CHARLES EDWIN[4] EDWARDS was born on 08 Nov 1925. He married Mary Ann Ramsey on 14 May 1949. She was born on 24 Jul 1929. She died in May 1979 in Houston, Texas.

8.   **ALLEN NEWTON[3] EDWARDS** (Isaac Mansfield[2], Ambrose Newton[1]) was born on 24 Apr 1902 in Texas. He died in Feb 1979 in Tulsa, Oklahoma. He married **ALLIE EDITH HERRIN**. She was born on 13 Feb 1905. She died in Feb 1991.

Allen Newton Edwards and Allie Edith Herrin had the following child:

      i. HOWARD KINDEL[4] EDWARDS was born on 25 Oct 1928 in Wichita County, Texas.

9.   **AMBROSE YARBROUGH[3] EDWARDS** (Ambrose Edwin[2], Ambrose Newton[1]) was born on 16 Sep 1904 in Greeneville, Texas. He died on 18 Mar 1999 in Dallas, Texas. He married Mary Ruth Howell, daughter of Zebbie Lee Howell and Laura Annie Middleton on 09 Aug 1935 in Greenville, Texas. She was born on 06 Sep 1905 in Richland, Texas. She died on 31 Dec 1998.

More About Ambrose Yarbrough Edwards:
Burial: Restland Cemetery, Dallas, Texas
Occupation: 1930; Accountant at automobile dealer, Greenville, Texas

More About Mary Ruth Howell:
Burial: Restland Cemetery, Dallas, Texas

Ambrose Yarbrough Edwards and Mary Ruth Howell had the following children:

20.   i. EDWIN LEE[4] EDWARDS was born on 17 Mar 1939 in Dallas, Texas. He married Anne Graham on 07 Aug 1965 in Atlanta, Georgia. She was born on 08 Aug 1940.

21.   ii. GEORGE AMBROSE EDWARDS was born on 29 Sep 1945 in Dallas, Texas. He married Marcia Jane Harms on 17 Jul 1976 in Houston, Texas. She was born on 06 May 1948.

10. **GEORGE NEWTON[3] EDWARDS** (Ambrose Edwin[2], Ambrose Newton[1]) was born on 01 May 1908 in Texas. He died on 28 Apr 1955 in University Park, Dallas County, Texas. He married **THERESA BRYAN**. She was born on 10 Sep 1907. She died on 29 Jul 1992.

More About George Newton Edwards:
Burial: 29 Apr 1955 in Restland Cemetery, Dallas,
Texas Cause Of Death: Malignant Brain Tumor
Occupation: Sales Representative

More About Theresa Bryan:
Burial: Restland Cemetery, Dallas, Texas

George Newton Edwards and Theresa Bryan had the following child:

      i. FRANCES ANN[4] EDWARDS was born on 14 Sep 1940 in Dallas County, Texas.

11. **MARION WIRT[3] EDWARDS** (McDonald[2], Ambrose Newton[1]) was born on 24 Aug 1901 in Strawn, Texas. He died on 07 Sep 1971 in Arlington, Tarrant County, Texas. He married Mary Elizabeth Gray on 30 Apr 1938 in Arlington, Texas. She was born on 18 Sep 1910 in Dallas, Texas. She died in 1999.

More About Marion Wirt Edwards:
Burial: 09 Sep 1971 in Moore Memorial Gardens, Arlington,
Texas
Cause Of Death: Cerebral Thrombosis
Occupation: City Secretary of Arlington, Texas
Occupation: Bookkeper for Vandergriff Chevrolet in Arlington, Texas
Occupation: Secretary - Treasurer for Midway Savings and Loan, Arlington, Texas

Marion Wirt Edwards and Mary Elizabeth Gray had the following children:

      i. BARBARA JEAN[4] EDWARDS was born on 17 Jul 1941 in Dallas County, Texas. She died in 2001.

          More About Barbara Jean Edwards:
          Cause Of Death: Brain Cancer

      ii. DONALD GRAY EDWARDS was born on 10 Jun 1944 in Dallas County, Texas.

22.   iii. CHARLES LEE EDWARDS was born on 18 Apr 1946 in Dallas County, Texas. He married PEGGY SHERIDAN.

12.   **ROY GARLAND[3] EDWARDS** (LeRoy Ardis[2], Ambrose Newton[1]) was born on 30 May 1922 in Loraine, Texas. He died on 14 Oct 1974 in Tampa, Florida. He married Maribel Savage, daughter of William Payne Savage and Mary Bell Badgett on 08 Apr 1944 in Lubbock, Texas. She was born on 22 Jun 1926 in Sherman, Texas. She died on 14 Feb 2010 in Tampa, Florida.

More About Roy Garland Edwards:
Burial: 17 Oct 1974 in Pleasant Grove Cemetery, Durant,
Florida Cause Of Death: Heart Failure
Occupation: 1940 in Olton, Texas; Repairman
Military Service: Bet. 1942-1964; U.S. Air Force (Major)

Notes for Roy Garland Edwards:
Died at the base hospital on MacDill Air Force Base.

More About Maribel Savage:
Burial: 18 Feb 2010 in Pleasant Grove Cemetery, Durant, Florida

Notes for Maribel Savage:
Born Mary Bell Savage but known as Maribel most of her life. Original birth certificate does not have a first name and amended birth certicate, filed June 20, 1952, has Maribel for her first name

Roy Garland Edwards and Maribel Savage had the following children:

23.   i. DAVID GARLAND[4] EDWARDS was born on 21 May 1945 in Fort Sumner, New Mexico. He married Hope Ellen Stewart, daughter of Robert McDaniel Stewart and Phyllis Olene Tucker on 09 Mar 1968 in Tampa, Florida. She was born on 27 Jun 1949 in South Perry, Ohio.

      ii. ROBERT MARION EDWARDS was born on 11 Dec 1946 in Lubbock, Texas. He died on 13 Feb 2010 in San Francisco, California. He met CATHERINE VLACHOS. She was born on 07 May 1950. She died on 17 Oct 2001 in San Francisco, California.

More About Robert Marion Edwards:
Cause Of Death: Lung Cancer

Notes for Robert Marion Edwards:
Never Married.

13. ESTHA LOUISE[3] EDWARDS (LeRoy Ardis[2], Ambrose Newton[1]) was born on 07 Apr 1908 in Ranger, Texas. She died on 23 May 1994 in Abilene, Texas. She married Floyd Franklin Coffee, son of Thomas Joshua Coffee and Hannah Pauline Dorn on 24 Aug 1934 in Snyder, Texas. He was born on 01 Dec 1900 in Mitchell County, Texas. He died on 19 Feb 1994 in Loraine, Texas.

More About Estha Louise
Edwards: Burial: Loraine, Texas
Occupation: 1930 in Loraine, Mitchell County, Texas; Public School Teacher

Notes for Estha Louise Edwards:
Head stone gives April 7, 1908 as birth date. Social Security Death Index gives April17, 1908 as birth date.

More About Floyd Franklin
Coffee: Burial: Loraine, Texas
Occupation: 1930 in Loraine, Texas; Grocery Store Merchant
Occupation: 1940 in Mitchell County, Texas; Farmer

More About Floyd Franklin Coffee and Estha Louise Edwards:
Marriage License: 24 Aug 1934 in Mitchell County, Texas
Marriage Fact: Married by S. H. Young, Methodist Minister

Floyd Franklin Coffee and Estha Louise Edwards had the following child:

24. i. PAULA JEAN[4] COFFEE was born on 11 May 1937 in Mitchell County, Texas. She died on 04 Aug 1998 in Taylor County, Texas. She married (1) WILLARD CALVIN BROCK, son of Hollis Milton Brock and Ruth Cummings on 10 Dec 1960 in Brownfield, Texas. He was born on 04 Feb 1928 in Denton County, Texas. He died on 21 Sep 1997 in Lubbock County, Texas. She married (2) CLINNON CAVON CARTWRIGHT, son of C.H. Cartwright and Aleene Beeman on 02 Mar 1956 in Loraine, Texas. He was born on 17 Apr 1936 in Nolan County, Texas. He died on 05 Apr 2003 in Colorado.

14. MARVIN YOUNG[3] EDWARDS (LeRoy Ardis[2], Ambrose Newton[1]) was born on 20 Sep 1910 in Alvin, Texas. He died on 19 Jan 1985 in Abilene, Texas. He married (1) EVELYN VIRGINIA COX, daughter of Bluford Sanford Cox and Mary Maud Baze on 15 Jun 1935 in Mitchell County, Texas. She was born on 11 May 1913 in Bay City, Texas. She died on 16 Feb 1979 in Abilene, Taylor County, Texas. He married (2) LAURA ALICE FERGUSON, daughter of Charles C. Ferguson and Annie Ruth Martin on 24 Sep 1981 in Jones County, Texas. She was born on 21 Sep 1919 in McCaulley, Fisher County, Texas. She died on 26 Jul 1994 in Abilene, Texas.

More About Marvin Young Edwards:
Burial: Elmwood Memorial Park, Abilene,
Texas Living In: 1940 Sweetwater, Texas
Occupation: 1930 in Loraine, Mitchell County, Texas; Lumber Yard Book Keeper
Occupation: 1940 in Sweetwater, Nolan County, Texas; Office Clerk in Morrison Supply Company

Military Service: Bet. 05 Nov 1943-03 Jan 1946; U. S. Navy

More About Evelyn Virginia Cox:
Burial: Elmwood Memorial Park, Abilene, Texas

More About Marvin Young Edwards and Evelyn Virginia Cox:
Marriage License: 15 Jun 1935 in Mitchell County, Texas
Marriage Fact: Married at M. E. Church South by Rev. C. B. Meadar

Marvin Young Edwards and Evelyn Virginia Cox had the following children:

25.   i. VIRGINIA CHARM[4] EDWARDS was born on 10 Dec 1936 in Sweetwater, Nolan County, Texas. She died on 14 May 1996 in San Angelo, Texas. She married (1) MILTON SHOBAL HOUSTON, son of Shobal Houston and Mary Lucy Notgrass on 18 Dec 1955 in Abilene, Texas. He was born on 14 Mar 1937 in Callahan County, Texas. He died on 13 Apr 1991 in Tom Green County, Texas. She married (2) DONALD WILLIAM SEWELL, son of Mailon Burke Sewell and Frances Virginia Cunningham on 01 Dec 1964. He was born on 11 Apr 1940. He died on 15 Feb 1996 in Abilene, Texas. She married (3) FRANK Y. MULTINE on 22 Aug 1981 in Jasper County, Texas. He was born about 1948.

26.   ii. JOHANNA EDWARDS was born on 16 Jan 1939 in Sweetwater, Texas. She married Charles Ray Bealmear, son of Clyde R. Bealmear and Audie Marre Hodo on 16 Jan 1959. He was born on 13 May 1932 in Dallas County, Texas.

More About Laura Alice Ferguson:
Burial: Elmwood Memorial Park, Abilene, Texas

Notes for Laura Alice Ferguson:
Texas death index has July 26, 1994 as date of death. Social Security death index has July 15, 1994 as date of death.

----

15.   **MARGARET RUTH[3] EDWARDS** (LeRoy Ardis[2], Ambrose Newton[1]) was born on 18 Jan 1917 in Loraine, Texas. She died on 26 Dec 1984 in Tempe, Arizona. She married William Glenn Johnson, son of Edgar Francis Johnson and Ada Eva Jennings on 25 Sep 1939 in Phoenix, Arizona. He was born on 12 Aug 1910 in Statesville, Tennessee. He died on 28 Jan 1988 in Tempe, Arizona.

More About William Glenn Johnson:
Occupation: 1940 in Tucson, Pima County, Arizona; Title Recorder in County Records Office

William Glenn Johnson and Margaret Ruth Edwards had the following children:

27.   i. MARGARET JOAN[4] JOHNSON was born on 09 Feb 1942 in Tucson, Arizona. She married Tommie Eugene Bain, son of Thomas Bain and Bertie Barnett on 02 May 1959 in Tucson, Arizona. He was born about 1938.

     ii. CAROL ANN JOHNSON was born on 07 Nov 1944 in Tucson, Arizona. She married JAMES MILLER RAY. She married WILLIAM KING.

16.   **RUTH[3] EDWARDS** (Becton Goodson[2], Ambrose Newton[1]) was born on 10 Aug 1912 in Tyler, Texas. She died on 05 Sep 2004 in Dallas, Texas. She married Albert Lee Greer in 1938. He was born on 4 Apr 1911 in Dallas, Texas. He died on 09 Nov 2001 in Dallas, Texas.

More About Ruth Edwards:

Burial: 09 Sep 2004 in Grove Hill Memorial Park, Dallas, Texas

Notes for Ruth Edwards:
GREER, RUTH EDWARDS, was born August 10, 1912 in Tyler, Texas to Becton G. and Minnie Mae Edwards. She passed away September 5, 2004 in Dallas, Texas. Ruth grew up in Forney, Texas, moving to Dallas in the early 30's. She was President of the PTA at Lakewood Elementary, J.L. Long Middle School, Woodrow Wilson High School, a longtime member of the East Dallas Ladies Kiwanis Club and a member of Highland Park United Methodist Church since 1940. For her entire adult life she was the glue that held a large extended family together. She was preceded in death by her husband, A.L. Greer. Survived by her daughter, Anne Greer Lasky of Dallas; son, Thomas Andrew Greer and his partner, Brian Falk of Taos, N.M.; sister, Margaret Robinson of Beaumont, Texas. Open visitation Tuesday, 12:00 - 9:00 P.M. at Sparkman/Hillcrest Funeral Home. Funeral services 2:00 P.M. Wednesday at Sparkman/Hillcrest Northwest Hwy. Chapel, Rev. Bill Smith, officiating. Interment to follow at Grove Hill Memorial Park. If desired, memorials may be made to the Lighthouse for the Blind, 4245 Office Parkway, Dallas, Texas 75204. Dignity Memorial Sparkman Hillcrest 7405 W. Northwest Hwy. Dallas (214) 363-5401

Published in Dallas Morning News from Sept. 6 to Sept. 7, 2004

Albert Lee Greer and Ruth Edwards had the following children:

28.   i. ANNE ELIZABETH[4] GREER was born on 26 Dec 1942 in Dallas County, Texas. She married SIDNEY LASKY. He was born on 03 Oct 1930 in Memphis, Tennessee. He died on 03 Jun 2003.

      ii. THOMAS ANDREW GREER was born on 10 Jan 1945 in Dallas County, Texas.

17.   **MARVIN BECTON[3] EDWARDS** (Becton Goodson[2], Ambrose Newton[1]) was born on 22 Nov 1923 in Texas. He died on 01 Feb 1973. He married Patricia Ann White on 25 Jun 1946 in Terrell County, Texas. She was born on 03 Mar 1928 in Terrell County, Texas. She died in Jan 2003 in Longview, Texas.

More About Marvin Becton Edwards:
Living In: 1961 Longview, Texas
Military Service: 04 Nov 1942 in Dallas, Dallas County, Texas; Enlisted in U.S. Army Air Force

Notes for Marvin Becton Edwards:
Served as navigator on a B-17. Was shot down near Dusseldorf, Germany and held as Prisoner of War for a year and a half.

Marvin Becton Edwards and Patricia Ann White had the following children:

29.   i. ROBERT WELDON[4] EDWARDS was born on 11 Nov 1949 in Travis County, Texas. He died on 15 Oct 1998 in Carbondale, Illinois. He married Molly Elizabeth Seale, daughter of James Seale and Ruby Conner on 15 Jun 1974 in Travis County, Texas. She was born on 07 Jan 1953 in Robertson County, Texas.

30.   ii. WILLIAM MATHEW EDWARDS was born on 05 Nov 1953 in Travis County, Texas. He married Lisa Lynn Roush on 27 Nov 1993 in Dallas County, Texas.

      iii. CAROL ELAINE EDWARDS was born on 02 Aug 1961 in Tarrant County, Texas.

31.   iv. CATHY LOU EDWARDS was born on 11 Dec 1962 in Tarrant County, Texas. She married (1) HAROLD KENT PARISH on 13 Sep 1986 in Gregg County, Texas. She married (2) JAMES RONALD NETHERLAND on 05 Jun 1993 in Dallas County, Texas.

        v. LINDA KAY EDWARDS was born on 11 Dec 1962 in Tarrant County, Texas.

18.   **MARGARET ANNE**[3] **EDWARDS** (Becton Goodson[2], Ambrose Newton[1]) was born on 04 Sep 1929 in Forney, Kaufman County, Texas. She died on 17 Jun 2011 in Silsbee, Texas. She married (1) **JOHN PATRICK MOONEYHAM**, son of Jesse Mooneyham and Hazel N. Easterly on 24 Sep 1947. He was born on 17 Mar 1929 in Kemp, Texas. He died on 23 Oct 2000 in Silsbee, Texas. She married (2) **ROBERT RAY ROBINSON** on 28 Feb 1981 in Jefferson County, Texas. He was born on 10 Jun 1944. He died on 28 Sep 2005 in Beaumont, Texas.

More About Margaret Anne Edwards:
Burial: 21 Jun 2011 in Forest Lawn Memorial Park Cemetery and Funeral Home, Beaumont, Texas

Notes for John Patrick Mooneyham:
Divorced from Margaret Anne Edwards on March 9, 1978.
Divorced from Betty J. Howell.

John Patrick Mooneyham and Margaret Anne Edwards had the following children:

32.   i. JOHN PATRICK[4] MOONEYHAM was born on 17 Nov 1948 in Dallas County, Texas. He married Sallie K. Hunt on 21 Nov 1969 in Jefferson County, Texas.

33.   ii. REBECCA ANNE MOONEYHAM was born on 03 Aug 1952 in Dallas County, Texas. She died on 20 Apr 1980 in Beaumont, Jefferson County, Texas. She married William M. Ramsey, son of Daniel Boone Ramsey on 23 Oct 1971 in Harris County, Texas. He was born on 21 Feb 1951.

More About Robert Ray Robinson:
Burial: 10 Oct 2005 in Forest Lawn Memorial Park Cemetery and Funeral Home, Beaumont, Texas Military Service: U.S. Army - Vietnam

Generation 4

19.   **CHARLES EDWIN**[4] **EDWARDS** (Murray Ardis[3], Isaac Mansfield[2], Ambrose Newton[1]) was born on 08 Nov 1925. He married Mary Ann Ramsey on 14 May 1949. She was born on 24 Jul 1929. She died in May 1979 in Houston, Texas.

Charles Edwin Edwards and Mary Ann Ramsey had the following child:

        i. CLIFFORD MURRAY[5] EDWARDS was born on 23 Sep 1952 in Tarrant County, Texas.

20.   **EDWIN LEE**[4] **EDWARDS** (Ambrose Yarbrough[3], Ambrose Edwin[2], Ambrose Newton[1]) was born on 17 Mar 1939 in Dallas, Texas. He married Anne Graham on 07 Aug 1965 in Atlanta, Georgia. She was born on 08 Aug 1940.

Edwin Lee Edwards and Anne Graham had the following children:

        i. GRAHAM LEE[5] EDWARDS was born on 10 Apr 1967.

        ii. MARK EDWIN EDWARDS was born on 31 Mar 1970.

21.   **GEORGE AMBROSE**[4] **EDWARDS** (Ambrose Yarbrough[3], Ambrose Edwin[2], Ambrose Newton[1]) was born on 29 Sep 1945 in Dallas, Texas. He married Marcia Jane Harms on 17 Jul 1976 in Houston, Texas. She was born on 06 May 1948.

George Ambrose Edwards and Marcia Jane Harms had the following children:

    i.   EMILY RUTH[5] EDWARDS was born on 13 Apr 1984 in Travis County, Texas.

    ii.   MARK ALAN EDWARDS was born on 30 Nov 1989 in Travis County, Texas.

22.   **CHARLES LEE[4] EDWARDS** (Marion Wirt[3], McDonald[2], Ambrose Newton[1]) was born on 18 Apr 1946 in Dallas County, Texas. He married **PEGGY SHERIDAN**.

More About Charles Lee Edwards:
Occupation: 1974; Worked for Shell Chemical Company and retired after thirty years.

More About Peggy Sheridan:
Occupation: Head Librarian at Houston Community College.

Charles Lee Edwards and Peggy Sheridan had the following children:

    i.   CHRISTOPHER LYNN[5] EDWARDS was born in 1980.

    ii.   KEVIN EDWARDS was born in 1984.

    iii.   MEGAN EDWARDS was born in 1987.

23.   **DAVID GARLAND[4] EDWARDS** (Roy Garland[3], LeRoy Ardis[2], Ambrose Newton[1]) was born on 21 May 1945 in Fort Sumner, New Mexico. He married Hope Ellen Stewart, daughter of Robert McDaniel Stewart and Phyllis Olene Tucker on 09 Mar 1968 in Tampa, Florida. She was born on 27 Jun 1949 in South Perry, Ohio.

More About David Garland Edwards:
Military Service: Bet. Nov 1965-Nov 1967; U.S. Army

David Garland Edwards and Hope Ellen Stewart had the following children:

34.   i. DIANA GAIL[5] EDWARDS was born on 28 Mar 1969 in Plant City, Florida. She married Mark Gregory Simmons on 23 Dec 1988 in Plant City, Florida. He was born on 29 Oct 1967.

35.   ii. DARLENE MARIE EDWARDS was born on 28 Dec 1970 in Plant City, Florida. She married Randall Edward Thompson, son of Larry Thompson and Jean Kennedy on 12 Sep 1993 in Pickerington, Ohio. He was born in 1970 in Indiana.

    iii. PATRICIA ANNE EDWARDS was born on 20 Oct 1972 in Plant City, Florida. She died on 20 Oct 1972 in Plant City, Florida.

More About Patricia Anne Edwards:
Burial: Pleasant Grove Cemetery, Durant, Florida

24.   **PAULA JEAN[4] COFFEE** (Estha Louise[3] Edwards, LeRoy Ardis[2] Edwards, Ambrose Newton[1] Edwards) was born on 11 May 1937 in Mitchell County, Texas. She died on 04 Aug 1998 in Taylor County, Texas. She married (1) **WILLARD CALVIN BROCK**, son of Hollis Milton Brock and Ruth Cummings on 10 Dec 1960 in Brownfield, Texas. He was born on 04 Feb 1928 in Denton County, Texas. He died on 21 Sep 1997 in Lubbock County, Texas. She married (2) **CLINNON CAVON CARTWRIGHT**, son of C.H. Cartwright and Aleene Beeman on 02 Mar 1956 in Loraine, Texas. He was born on 17 Apr 1936 in Nolan County, Texas. He died on 05 Apr 2003 in Colorado.

More About Paula Jean Coffee:
Burial: Loraine Cemetery, Loraine, Texas

Notes for Paula Jean Coffee:
 THE ABILENE REPORTER-NEWS Abliene, Texas. Sunday Morning, March 4, 1956. TO LIVE IN LUBBOCK. Paula Jean Coffee Becomes bride of Clinnon Cartwright. LORAINE, March 3. Paula Jean Coffee, daughter of Mr. and Mrs. Floyd Coffee, became the bride of Clinnon Cavon Cartwright of Lubbock, in the First Methodist Church Friday evening. The bridegroom is the son of Mr. and Mrs. C. H. Cartwright of Sweetwater. The Rev. T. L. Darby, pastor. Ushers were Ralph B. Mabry, Max Keating and Jack D. Nachinger, all of Lubbock, and Jimmy Hall of Abilene. The bride's father gave her in marriage. She wore a dress of chantilly lace and tulle over satin. The bodice and neckline were re-embroidered with chantilly lace and seed pearl. She carried a white satin covered Bible in a double ring ceremony. Baskets of white stocks and gladioli, with a background of greenery and candelabra decorated the altar. Mrs. K. L. Taylor, organist, accompanied Ann Herrihgton of Carrizo Springs, who sang "Because" and "The Lord's Prayer." Delbert Hess of Hermleigh was best man and Mrs. Milton Houston of Abilene, cousin of the bride, was matron of honor. Bridesmaids were Jackie Coffee and Johahnah Edwards of Abilene, both cousins of the bride. Jimmy Hall of Abilene and Ralph B. Mabry of Lubbock, lighted the candles. The matron of honor and bridesmaids wore dresses of ice blue crystaieiie, made princess style. They wore matching rnitts and net halo hats. Their nosegays were of white carnations with touches of blue. A reception was held in the bride's parents home. Guests attended from Abilene, Lubbock, Roscoe, Sweetwater, Hermleigh, Midland, Carrizo Springs and Colorado City. The bride's table was laid with white linen and decorated in the chosen colors of blue and white. The attendants' bouquets were used to form a centerpiece. Silver and crystal appointments and a three tiered wedding cake completed decorations. Joy Smith of Sweetwater registered guests. Others in the house- party were Bobbie Motes, Pricilla Givens, Beverly Johnson and Wanda Wells. After a wedding trip the couple will live in Lubbock at 2321 l5th St. For a trip to Buchanan Lake, the bride wore a beige suit and matching duster. Her accessories were brown and yellow and she wore a corsage from the bridal bouquet. The bride was graduated from Loraine High School and attended McMurry College in Abilene. The bridegroom was graduated from Sweetwater High, Schol and is a sophomore at Texas Technological College. Both plan to continue their education at the Lubbock college.

More About Willard Calvin Brock:
Burial: Loraine Cemetery, Loraine, Texas

Willard Calvin Brock and Paula Jean Coffee had the following child:

36. i. ROBERT PAUL[5] BROCK was born on 01 Sep 1964 in Texas. He married (1) LEAH ANETTA MCBRIDE, daughter of Auvy Lee McBride and Leslie Anita Nichols on 20 Jan 1989 in Gaines County, Texas. She was born on 17 Oct 1960 in Lubbock, Texas. He married (2) MARIA TRISTANA on 13 Jun 1998 in Hazelwood, Missouri. She was born about 1962.

More About Clinnon Cavon Cartwright:
Occupation: 1957 in Lubbock, Texas; Warehouseman
Occupation: 1958 in Lubbock, Texas; Salesman
Occupation: 1959 in Lubbock, Texas; Agent for Continental Airlines
Occupation: 1960 in Lubbock, Texas; Agent for Continental Airlines

25. VIRGINIA CHARM[4] EDWARDS (Marvin Young[3], LeRoy Ardis[2], Ambrose Newton[1]) was born on 10 Dec 1936 in Sweetwater, Nolan County, Texas. She died on 14 May 1996 in San Angelo, Texas. She married (1) MILTON SHOBAL HOUSTON, son of Shobal Houston and Mary Lucy Notgrass on 18 Dec 1955 in Abilene, Texas. He was born on 14 Mar 1937 in Callahan County, Texas. He died on 13 Apr 1991 in Tom Green County, Texas. She married (2) DONALD WILLIAM SEWELL, son of Mailon

Burke Sewell and Frances Virginia Cunningham on 01 Dec 1964. He was born on 11 Apr 1940. He died on 15 Feb 1996 in Abilene, Texas. She married (3) **FRANK Y. MULTINE** on 22 Aug 1981 in Jasper County, Texas. He was born about 1948.

More About Virginia Charm Edwards:
Burial: Old Cottonwood Cemetery, Cottonwood, Callahan County, Texas

Milton Shobal Houston and Virginia Charm Edwards had the following children:

37.　　i. MILTON CARY[5] HOUSTON was born on 25 Sep 1957 in Abilene, Texas. He married Carla Sue Rose on 06 Jan 1979 in San Angelo, Texas.

38.　　ii. CYNTHIA ANN HOUSTON was born on 17 Sep 1960 in Abilene, Texas. She married David Brian Michael, son of Paul Michael and Marna Sullivan on 24 Jun 1984 in San Angelo, Texas.

Donald William Sewell and Virginia Charm Edwards had the following children:

39.　　i. LORI KAY[5] SEWELL was born on 30 Dec 1964 in Abilene, Texas. She married Kenneth Wayne Hollingsworth, son of Kenneth Hollingsworth on 15 Mar 1986 in San Angelo, Texas.

　　ii. DONATHAN ARDIS SEWELL was born on 12 Sep 1966 in Abilene, Texas.

More About Donathan Ardis Sewell:
Occupation: Firefighter
Military Service: U.S. Marines

40.　　iii. DANIEL SEWELL was born on 26 May 1968 in Cleburne, Johnson County, Texas. He married Frances Ann Holmes on 17 Feb 1990 in Casa Grande, Arizona.

26.　**JOHANNA[4] EDWARDS** (Marvin Young[3], LeRoy Ardis[2], Ambrose Newton[1]) was born on 16 Jan 1939 in Sweetwater, Texas. She married Charles Ray Bealmear, son of Clyde R. Bealmear and Audie Marre Hodo on 16 Jan 1959. He was born on 13 May 1932 in Dallas County, Texas.

Charles Ray Bealmear and Johanna Edwards had the following children:

41.　　i. KIMBERLY DEANN[5] BEALMEAR was born on 09 Aug 1962 in Dallas, Texas. She married Carl Alan Carter on 23 Nov 1985 in Lubbock, Texas. He was born on 11 Nov 1985 in Nueces County, Texas.

　　ii. MICHELLE MARIE BEALMEAR was born on 12 May 1964 in Karlsrue, Germany.

　　iii. CHARLES RODNEY BEALMEAR was born on 28 Jun 1969 in Dallas County, Texas. He died on 29 Dec 1988 in Chicago, Illinois.

More About Charles Rodney Bealmear:
Burial: Restland Memorial Park, Dallas, Dallas County, Texas Military Service: United States Navy

27.　**MARGARET JOAN[4] JOHNSON** (Margaret Ruth[3] Edwards, LeRoy Ardis[2] Edwards, Ambrose Newton[1] Edwards) was born on 09 Feb 1942 in Tucson, Arizona. She married Tommie Eugene Bain, son of Thomas Bain and Bertie Barnett on 02 May 1959 in Tucson, Arizona. He was born about 1938.

Tommie Eugene Bain and Margaret Joan Johnson had the following child:

42.   i. TOMMIE GLENN[5] BAIN was born on 24 Mar 1961 in Long Beach, California. He married (1) TERESA LEILANI MCELROY, daughter of James McElroy on 30 May 1981 in Phoenix, Arizona. He married (2) MICHELE LEE ARCHER, daughter of Jon Archer and Virginia Halahurick on 14 Feb 1997 in Norfolk, Virginia.

28. **ANNE ELIZABETH[4] GREER** (Ruth[3] Edwards, Becton Goodson[2] Edwards, Ambrose Newton[1] Edwards) was born on 26 Dec 1942 in Dallas County, Texas. She married **SIDNEY LASKY**. He was born on 03 Oct 1930 in Memphis, Tennessee. He died on 03 Jun 2003.

Sidney Lasky and Anne Elizabeth Greer had the following child:

    i. SARAH GREER[5] LASKY was born on 01 Aug 1974 in Dallas County, Texas.

29. **ROBERT WELDON[4] EDWARDS** (Marvin Becton[3], Becton Goodson[2], Ambrose Newton[1]) was born on 11 Nov 1949 in Travis County, Texas. He died on 15 Oct 1998 in Carbondale, Illinois. He married Molly Elizabeth Seale, daughter of James Seale and Ruby Conner on 15 Jun 1974 in Travis County, Texas. She was born on 07 Jan 1953 in Robertson County, Texas.

More About Robert Weldon Edwards:
Burial: 17 Oct 1998 in Carbondale, Illinois

Robert Weldon Edwards and Molly Elizabeth Seale had the following children:

    i. JAMES MARVIN[5] EDWARDS was born on 30 Aug 1982 in Travis County, Texas.

    ii. CHARLES BECTON EDWARDS was born on 11 Nov 1985 in Travis County, Texas.

30. **WILLIAM MATHEW[4] EDWARDS** (Marvin Becton[3], Becton Goodson[2], Ambrose Newton[1]) was born on 05 Nov 1953 in Travis County, Texas. He married Lisa Lynn Roush on 27 Nov 1993 in Dallas County, Texas.

William Mathew Edwards and Lisa Lynn Roush had the following children:

    i. MARK WILLIAM[5] EDWARDS was born on 12 Apr 1994 in Dallas County, Texas.

        Notes for Mark William Edwards:
        Twin brother of Eric Edwards.

    ii. ERIC ROBERT EDWARDS was born on 12 Apr 1994 in Dallas County, Texas.

        Notes for Eric Robert Edwards:
        Twin brother of Mark Edwards.

31. **CATHY LOU[4] EDWARDS** (Marvin Becton[3], Becton Goodson[2], Ambrose Newton[1]) was born on 11 Dec 1962 in Tarrant County, Texas. She married (1) **HAROLD KENT PARISH** on 13 Sep 1986 in Gregg County, Texas. She married (2) **JAMES RONALD NETHERLAND** on 05 Jun 1993 in Dallas County, Texas.

Harold Kent Parish and Cathy Lou Edwards had the following children:

    i. MICHAEL KENT[5] PARISH was born on 03 Jun 1987 in Gregg County, Texas.

    ii. LOGAN KANE PARISH was born on 06 Dec 1990 in Dallas County, Texas.

James Ronald Netherland and Cathy Lou Edwards had the following child:

    i.   JAMES HUNTER[5] NETHERLAND was born on 22 Jan 1994 in Dallas County, Texas.

32.   JOHN PATRICK[4] MOONEYHAM (Margaret Anne[3] Edwards, Becton Goodson[2] Edwards, Ambrose Newton[1] Edwards) was born on 17 Nov 1948 in Dallas County, Texas. He married Sallie K. Hunt on 21 Nov 1969 in Jefferson County, Texas.

John Patrick Mooneyham and Sallie K. Hunt had the following children:

    i.   JOHN PATRICK[5] MOONEYHAM was born on 19 Sep 1975.

    ii.   RYAN MITCHUM MOONEYHAM was born on 30 Jun 1981.

33.   REBECCA ANNE[4] MOONEYHAM (Margaret Anne[3] Edwards, Becton Goodson[2] Edwards, Ambrose Newton[1] Edwards) was born on 03 Aug 1952 in Dallas County, Texas. She died on 20 Apr 1980 in Beaumont, Jefferson County, Texas. She married William M. Ramsey, son of Daniel Boone Ramsey on 23 Oct 1971 in Harris County, Texas. He was born on 21 Feb 1951.

More About Rebecca Anne Mooneyham:
Burial: Forest Lawn Memorial Park Cemetery and Funeral Home, Beaumont, Texas

William M. Ramsey and Rebecca Anne Mooneyham had the following children:

43.   i. SCOTT WILLIAM[5] RAMSEY was born on 01 Feb 1973 in Beaumont, Texas. He married Anna Harriet Blinn in 2002. She was born on 17 Feb 1962 in Huntington Station, New York.

    ii.   JULIE ANNE RAMSEY was born on 01 Mar 1978. She married TIM WEEKLY.

Generation 5

34.   DIANA GAIL[5] EDWARDS (David Garland[4], Roy Garland[3], LeRoy Ardis[2], Ambrose Newton[1]) was born on 28 Mar 1969 in Plant City, Florida. She married Mark Gregory Simmons on 23 Dec 1988 in Plant City, Florida. He was born on 29 Oct 1967.

Mark Gregory Simmons and Diana Gail Edwards had the following children:

44.   i. MARK GREGORY[6] EDWARDS was born on 20 Jun 1988 in Plant City, Florida. He married Julie Ann Mercer on 17 Feb 2007 in Wellston, Ohio. She was born on 28 May 1988.

45.   ii. DAVIAN GAIL SIMMONS was born on 12 Feb 1991 in Monroe, North Carolina. She married Jerrod Elden Rogers, son of James J. Rogers and Betty Lou Eberts on 24 Mar 2012 in Jackson County, Ohio. He was born on 17 Mar 1987 in Ohio.

35.   DARLENE MARIE[5] EDWARDS (David Garland[4], Roy Garland[3], LeRoy Ardis[2], Ambrose Newton[1]) was born on 28 Dec 1970 in Plant City, Florida. She married Randall Edward Thompson, son of Larry Thompson and Jean Kennedy on 12 Sep 1993 in Pickerington, Ohio. He was born in 1970 in Indiana.

Randall Edward Thompson and Darlene Marie Edwards had the following children:

    i.   TREVOR NATHANIEL[6] THOMPSON was born on 11 Sep 1995 in Ohio.

    ii.   VICTORIA KATHLEEN THOMPSON was born in Mar 1997 in Ohio. She married Keegan Coldiron on 12 Aug 2016.

36.   ROBERT PAUL[5] BROCK (Paula Jean[4] Coffee, Estha Louise[3] Edwards, LeRoy Ardis[2] Edwards, Ambrose Newton[1] Edwards) was born on 01 Sep 1964 in Texas. He married (1) LEAH ANETTA

MCBRIDE, daughter of Auvy Lee McBride and Leslie Anita Nichols on 20 Jan 1989 in Gaines County, Texas. She was born on 17 Oct 1960 in Lubbock, Texas. He married (2) **MARIA TRISTANA** on 13 Jun 1998 in Hazelwood, Missouri. She was born about 1962.

Robert Paul Brock and Maria Tristana had the following child:

    i.   CHRISTOPHER MICHAEL^6 BROCK was born on 31 Oct 1999.

37.   **MILTON CARY^5 HOUSTON** (Virginia Charm^4 Edwards, Marvin Young^3 Edwards, LeRoy Ardis^2 Edwards, Ambrose Newton^1 Edwards) was born on 25 Sep 1957 in Abilene, Texas. He married Carla Sue Rose on 06 Jan 1979 in San Angelo, Texas.

Milton Cary Houston and Carla Sue Rose had the following children:

    i.   CHRISTY AARON^6 HOUSTON was born on 26 Sep 1981 in Brazos County, Texas.

    ii.   CAREY ANN HOUSTON was born on 14 Oct 1983 in Taylor County, Texas.

    iii.   COURTNEY ALYCE HOUSTON was born on 15 Feb 1988 in Tom Green county, Texas.

    iv.   COREY ALLISON HOUSTON was born on 19 Jun 1989 in Tom Green county, Texas.

    v.   CASEY ANNETTE HOUSTON was born on 04 Jul 1997 in Tom Green county, Texas.

38.   **CYNTHIA ANN^5 HOUSTON** (Virginia Charm^4 Edwards, Marvin Young^3 Edwards, LeRoy Ardis^2 Edwards, Ambrose Newton^1 Edwards) was born on 17 Sep 1960 in Abilene, Texas. She married David Brian Michael, son of Paul Michael and Marna Sullivan on 24 Jun 1984 in San Angelo, Texas.

David Brian Michael and Cynthia Ann Houston had the following children:

    i.   JOSEPH ANTHONE^6 MICHAEL was born on 13 Jan 1981.

    ii.   STEPHANIE DIANA MICHAEL was born on 09 Jan 1982.

    iii.   SEAN PATRICK MICHAEL was born on 04 Feb 1985.

    iv.   SARAH ALYSE MICHAEL was born on 19 Feb 1987.

    v.   JUSTON PAUL MICHAEL was born on 27 Jun 1990.

39.   **LORI KAY^5 SEWELL** (Virginia Charm^4 Edwards, Marvin Young^3 Edwards, LeRoy Ardis^2 Edwards, Ambrose Newton^1 Edwards) was born on 30 Dec 1964 in Abilene, Texas. She married Kenneth Wayne Hollingsworth, son of Kenneth Hollingsworth on 15 Mar 1986 in San Angelo, Texas.

Kenneth Wayne Hollingsworth and Lori Kay Sewell had the following children:

    i.   CHANDICE ANN^6 HOLLINGSWORTH was born on 20 Feb 1987 in Tom Green county, Texas.

    ii.   KENNETH ANDREW HOLLINGSWORTH was born on 07 Dec 1989 in Tom Green county, Texas.

40.   **DANIEL^5 SEWELL** (Virginia Charm^4 Edwards, Marvin Young^3 Edwards, LeRoy Ardis^2 Edwards, Ambrose Newton^1 Edwards) was born on 26 May 1968 in Cleburne, Johnson County, Texas. He married Frances Ann Holmes on 17 Feb 1990 in Casa Grande, Arizona.

Daniel Sewell and Frances Ann Holmes had the following children:

    i.   DONITHAN SCOTT[6] SEWELL was born on 04 Dec 1990.

    ii.   ZANE EDWARDS SEWELL was born on 21 Feb 1993.

    iii.   TY DANIEL SEWELL was born on 31 Jan 1995.

41.   **KIMBERLY DEANN[5] BEALMEAR** (Johanna[4] Edwards, Marvin Young[3] Edwards, LeRoy Ardis[2] Edwards, Ambrose Newton[1] Edwards) was born on 09 Aug 1962 in Dallas, Texas. She married Carl Alan Carter on 23 Nov 1985 in Lubbock, Texas. He was born on 11 Nov 1985 in Nueces County, Texas.

More About Kimberly Deann Bealmear:
Occupation: Operating Room Nurse

Carl Alan Carter and Kimberly Deann Bealmear had the following child:

    i.   KRISTINA RENEE[6] CARTER was born on 25 Aug 1990 in Dallas, Texas.

42.   **TOMMIE GLENN[5] BAIN** (Margaret Joan[4] Johnson, Margaret Ruth[3] Edwards, LeRoy Ardis[2] Edwards, Ambrose Newton[1] Edwards) was born on 24 Mar 1961 in Long Beach, California. He married (1) **TERESA LEILANI MCELROY**, daughter of James McElroy on 30 May 1981 in Phoenix, Arizona. He married (2) **MICHELE LEE ARCHER**, daughter of Jon Archer and Virginia Halahurick on 14 Feb 1997 in Norfolk, Virginia.

Tommie Glenn Bain and Teresa Leilani McElroy had the following children:

    i.   TOMMIE JAMES[6] BAIN was born on 17 May 1983.

    ii.   JONATHON ADAM BAIN was born on 21 Sep 1984.

    iii.   JOSHUA DANIEL BAIN was born on 29 Sep 1986.

    iv.   STEVEN PHILLIP BAIN was born on 10 Dec 1987.

    v.   CHRISTOPHER JUSTIN BAIN was born on 01 Sep 1990.

43.   **SCOTT WILLIAM[5] RAMSEY** (Rebecca Anne[4] Mooneyham, Margaret Anne[3] Edwards, Becton Goodson[2] Edwards, Ambrose Newton[1] Edwards) was born on 01 Feb 1973 in Beaumont, Texas. He married Anna Harriet Blinn in 2002. She was born on 17 Feb 1962 in Huntington Station, New York.

Notes for Scott William Ramsey:
Children are from previous marriages.

Scott William Ramsey and Anna Harriet Blinn had the following children:

    i.   CLAYTON MITCHELL[6] RAMSEY was born on 04 Oct 1996 in San Diego, California.

    ii.   ADRIANE MARIE BLINN was born on 21 May 1984 in Hudson, New York.

    iii.   JONATHAN ROBERT BLINN was born on 03 Jul 1985 in Hudson, New York.

Generation 6

44.   **MARK GREGORY**[6] **EDWARDS** (Diana Gail[5], David Garland[4], Roy Garland[3], LeRoy Ardis[2], Ambrose Newton[1]) was born on 20 Jun 1988 in Plant City, Florida. He married Julie Ann Mercer on 17 Feb 2007 in Wellston, Ohio. She was born on 28 May 1988.

Mark Gregory Edwards and Julie Ann Mercer had the following children:

    i.   SOPHIA MARIE[7] EDWARDS was born on 05 Aug 2010 in Chillicothe, Ohio.

    ii.   MARK WILTON EDWARDS was born on 28 Oct 2013 in Columbus, Ohio.

45.   **DAVIAN GAIL**[6] **SIMMONS** (Diana Gail[5] Edwards, David Garland[4] Edwards, Roy Garland[3] Edwards, LeRoy Ardis[2] Edwards, Ambrose Newton[1] Edwards) was born on 12 Feb 1991 in Monroe, North Carolina. She married Jerrod Elden Rogers, son of James J. Rogers and Betty Lou Eberts on 24 Mar 2012 in Jackson County, Ohio. He was born on 17 Mar 1987 in Ohio.

More About Jerrod Elden Rogers and Davian Gail Simmons:
Marriage Fact: Married in Grace Baptist Fellowship Church, Berlin Crossroads,
Ohio Marriage Fact: Married by Timothy L. Jones, MG.

Jerrod Elden Rogers and Davian Gail Simmons had the following children:

    i.   DAVID[7] ROGERS was born on 03 May 2014 in Athens, Ohio.

    ii.   CLOE GAIL ROGERS was born on 14 May 2016 in Athens, Ohio.